EXTINCTION REBELLION

Poems by

Geza Tatrallyay

Copyright© 2020 Geza Tatrallyay
ISBN: 978-93-90202-32-4

First Edition: 2020
Rs. 200/- $ 15

Cyberwit.net
HIG 45 Kaushambi Kunj, Kalindipuram
Allahabad - 211011 (U.P.) India
http://www.cyberwit.net
Tel: +(91) 9415091004 +(91) (532) 2552257
E-mail: info@cyberwit.net

Printed at Repro India Limited.

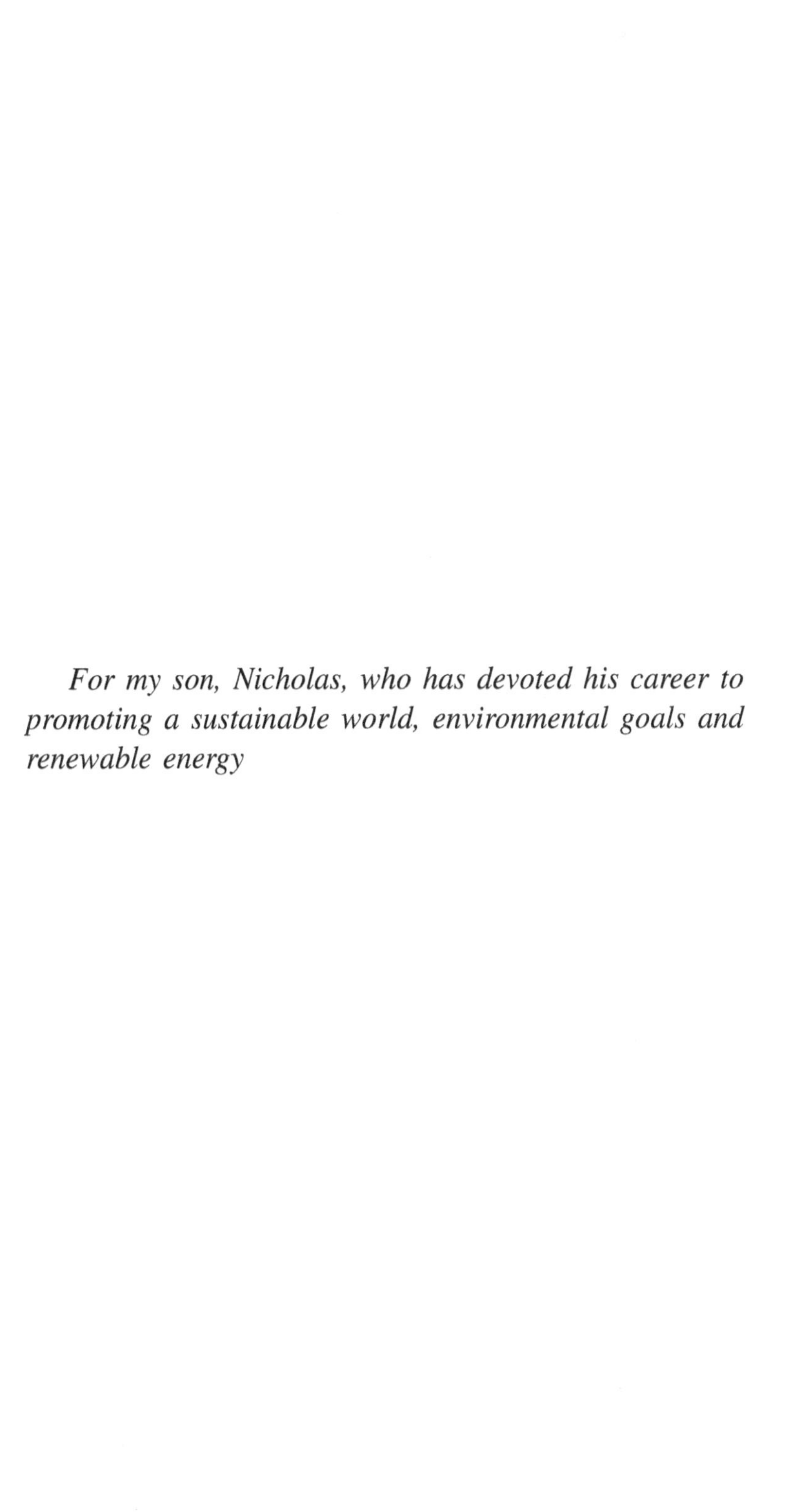

For my son, Nicholas, who has devoted his career to promoting a sustainable world, environmental goals and renewable energy

Acknowledgements

The poems *Pollination* and *There are too many of us on this earth* ... appear in the 2020 *PoemTown Anthology* put out by the town of Randolph VT.

The poem, *The Hare*, has been published in Volume LXVI of *The Mountain Troubadour*, 2020.

Foreword

Geza Tatrallyay calls out a warning in this collection. From the title through the last poem, he warns us to listen to our children and listen to the earth. His warning cries address species extinction, climate change and pandemic. In these succinct verses he joins the most prescient poets, writers like Marge Piercy and Robinson Jeffers. Our leaders have failed us and the environment, he tells us. His words are heart-wrenching and hard to read. These poems are biblical in cadence, poignant and succinct warning cries offset by sensitivity to the earth and its creatures. Here is a poet who can warn us of hellfire. Here is a poet who speaks for earth's maligned and ignored creatures: a coyote, a turtle, a snake, an earthworm. Read these poems and weep. Read these poems and rejoice in their call to conscience and action.

George Longenecker

President

Poetry Society of Vermont

Introduction

Extinction Rebellion is my fourth collection of poems. The first three, *Cello's Tears, Sighs and Murmurs* and *Extinction*, were published by P.R.A. Publishing, a respectable small publisher from Georgia, USA. They have been a delight to work with and I am grateful for their support. I am very pleased that Cyberwit, the internationally renowned publisher of poetry has decided to publish this fourth collection, *Extinction Rebellion*.

This volume is the second one with the theme of climate change and extinction and, as in *Extinction*, most of the poems indeed tackle the topic of environmental destruction and the resulting possible disappearance of species, including mankind. Several recent reports by agencies of the United Nations and different groups of concerned scientists detail the heightened risks mankind is facing due to continued use of fossil fuels and the resulting greenhouse gas emissions. The coronavirus pandemic is yet another signal from nature that mankind's burden may be simply too much. With the angry protests targeting inaction by our politicians and business leaders, launched by Greta Thunberg and the Extinction Rebellion movement, it is imperative that we all speak up and act. First my previous collection, *Extinction,* and now *Extinction Rebellion* are some of my own small contributions to these efforts.

I have divided the poems into four parts. **Part I, The World**, deals with climate change and its impact on mother earth and humanity. **Part II, Species,** takes a look at what this destruction of the environment is doing to life around us, to individual species of animals and plants. It includes some of what I call my "beastie" poems—and I have written quite a few of these, spread over all four of my poetry collections— many of which were inspired by contact with, or concern for, a particular species of life. **Part III, Mankind,** are poems that key in on humanity's role in this destruction and our possible fate as a result of our collective actions. **Part IV, Pandemic,** brings into focus the tragedy of the devastating spread of the coronavirus across the globe.

My readers will perceive that my poems tend to be short and succinct: my particular view of good poetry is that it should be sparing in the use of words to paint a picture or capture an emotion. Hence my love of the *haiku* form which I became fascinated with when I lived in Japan in my early twenties. Indeed, I have chosen to end each section with a number of poems written in this form.

I hope you, my reader, will enjoy these poems and that they may spur you to action!

Geza Tatrallyay

Barnard VT

Contents

III. Mankind

I. The World

I often wonder when I see …

I often wonder when I see
the hate-filled, calamitous world,
the wars, the bombings, the famine,
the legacy we leave behind—
what lives will my grandchildren have,
my children, too, how will they cope?

I often wonder when I see
this ever-more polluted earth,
the poisoned potable water,
the acrid yellow air we breathe—
how will my grandchildren survive,
my children, too, will they adapt?

I often wonder when I see
the crowding in big city slums,
the masses escaping terror,
persecution, murder and rape—
will my children be able to survive,
my grandchildren, will they endure?

Frolicking flames

The frolicking flames of hellfire
devour our primeval forests:
we burn filthy fossil fuels,
spewing into the air gases
that trap the sun's heat, warming earth,
causing drought that scorches the land
and melting the polar ice cap—
sea levels rise, flooding our towns
eroding beaches, wasting floodplains—
we are destroying mother earth
and much of life that lives on it,
including our conceited selves.

Finally it rained again in the night

Finally it rained again in the night,
drops of water falling from the heavens
wetting the cracked earth, turning it to mud

Finally it rained again in the night,
extinguishing the flames of forest fires
that scorched the land and burned all in the way

Finally it rained again in the night,
reinvigorating withering roots,
bequeathing renewed life to plants and trees

Finally it rained again in the night,
filling former lakes and dried-up rivers,
securing succor for parched animals

Finally it rained again in the night,
replenishing depleted reservoirs,
giving hope to those fearing future thirst

Finally it rained again in the night:
when will it pour again for days on end,
when will this intolerable drought end?

Detritus desecrates the land ...

Detritus desecrates the land,
our plastics suffocate the seas,
chemical flatulence, the air—
we consciously choose to pollute,
pursuing consumptive pleasure,
propelling our own extinction.

We exist in four dimensions

We exist in four dimensions—
that is, at least we think we do—
where time ticks relentlessly by
and we mortals bulge into space
until the black hole hijacks us
and our world simply expires

Polar vortex

A blinding blizzard blows:
the polar vortex split—
snow and ice rule the world.
When will spring come again?

The universe whirls on …

A donut-like black hole
swallowed the sun today
and had us for dessert:
the universe whirls on,
timeless and infinite

We just cower in the cellar

Drought cracks the soil, withers our crops
fires burn our forests, scorch our fields
gale force winds scour the landscape—
drenching rain and the rising seas
flood our towns, wash away the coast,
mudslides bury whole villages—
the blighted earth is fighting back
and frightened at what we have done,
we just cower in the cellar

The stream slips by

The stream slips by
from source to sea,
like human life,
from birth to death

Clean water

Clean water,
so vital,
so scarce—

I die of thirst

A hurricane

A hurricane lashes the low-lying island
with unrelenting, punishing ferocity:
violent winds tear up trees, rip apart buildings—
the tidal surge rises, a giant sea monster
that invades the land, washing everything away:
man and his creations, all fruits of evolution—

and when the storm passes, devastation remains:
the sun shines only on carrion and corpses—
remnants of lives, of homes, of cities, of forests,
a frying pan, a soggy book, a doll's torso,
maybe a roof tile and a twisted vehicle,
fallen streetlights, broken windows, an unpaired boot—

then, with lots of tears, the cleanup and rebuild start,
until the next cyclone comes to chastise us again

The fog is rolling in ...

The fog is rolling in
across the waveless bay,
obscuring the far shore—

except the mountaintops
that float freely in space,
while white cotton candy
spreads across the water,
eerie and ominous—

Could it be portending
Gaia's retribution
for mankind's mindlessness,
the uncaring ravaging
of her magnificence?

Will there still be water

The waterfall weeps tears that fly down the rock face
in myriads of perfect miniscule globules
inhabited by microscopic forms of life:
viruses and bacteria and other nano-beings—

water, the substance that nourishes all nature,
including man, that self-centered, destructive beast
who wantonly wastes this precious vital resource
that may in fact only exist on our planet

will there still be water on earth to nurture life
in its hardier, minute less demanding forms,
when we are no longer, when mankind is extinct—
and not just to weep tears for our fatal folly?

Haiku: the sky weeps with woe

the sky weeps with woe:
we have polluted the air,
the land and the sea

Haiku: the man in the moon

the man in the moon
sees the smog clogging our air:
he laments our fate

Haiku: is there no way out?

Is there no way out?
we have messed up the planet
and face extinction

Haiku: the earth cries for us

the earth cries for us,
the callous ones who trash it:
we will not survive

II. Species

How many species will survive?

How many species will survive
the destruction we have unleashed
on our planet's ecosystems?
China builds coal-fired power plants;
India too, despite bad air—
we cannot stop powering our
lives by burning fossil fuels.
In Brazil, the Amazon burns,
drought devastates Australia
and other regions of the world.
The polar ice cap is melting;
violent storms, wind and rain
are causing sea levels to rise,
flooding our coastal cities,
our fragile shore ecosystems.
As harvests fail, food becomes scarce,
potable water is poisoned
with agricultural runoff
and corporate chemical spills.
We must step back and change our ways:
we must give first priority
to the health of our mother earth.

Will I still be alive?

I am the sinewy buck
that stalks through the forest

I am the vicious wolf
that bares its incisors

I am the wide-winged eagle
that soars above the land

I am the hummingbird
that buzzes the bee balm

I am the sockeye salmon
that saults up waterfalls

I am the princess frog
that jumps in the water

I am the cicada
that plays the night fiddle

I am the mosquito
that bites you and your friend

I am the vile virus
that causes you to die

I am the foul maggot
that eats carrion flesh

will I still be alive
after your killing kind?

Where the lemons blossom ...

(Wo die Zitronen blühen ...)

Lemons still blossom, and not just in Italy—
they thrive in Assam, in Burma and Persia,
as well, in California and Florida.
You can hear Strauss's *"Wo die Zitronen blühen"* waltz
today on your iPhone anywhere in the world
or read the novel by Johann Wolfgang von Goethe,
his masterpiece, *"Wilhelm Meister's Apprenticeship"*,
you can delight in Manet's exquisite still life,
"Le Citron", painted in eighteen hundred and eighty.
But will lemons—will anything—still bloom anywhere
when man-caused climate change ravages this planet?
Will we be around to appreciate this fruit,
so perfect: its blossom's beauty, its taste's tartness,
and the wonder of the sublime art it inspired?

Pollination

A bumblebee buzzes by the bee balm
seeking the blossoms' sweet nectar to suck
with its protracted straw-like proboscis—

inadvertently, it picks up pollen,
brushes it into its corbicula,
packing the fine dust and the propolis
with the pollen press on its hind legs

when the bee alights on the next flower
some of the golden powder brushes off
on the fertile pistil's sticky stigma,
completing magical pollination

next summer's sun will bring forth new blossoms
and bumblebees will pollinate yet again—
unless … unless, our polluting poisons
devastate their dwindling population.

The chiding cricket

I was dozing spread-eagled on the grass,
when a cricket catapulted onto my crotch,
wiggled its antenna and chided me,
admonishing me for mankind's folly—

yes, the brazen creature took me to task
for our uncaring, polluting lifestyle,
our devastation of its habitat.

I had nothing to say in our defense.

Daddy long legs

a daddy long legs was scrambling on the screen door,
seeming of fragile construction, easy to crush,
daresay, a delicate creature, with eight splayed limbs,
a puff of wind might blow this skull spider away—

but these arachnids are a wonder of nature,
surviving, unchanged for three hundred million years—
better endowed than we, with three pairs of peepers,
they vibrate rapidly to confound predators
and throw their silken web on their mosquito prey

these spiders could teach us peaceful coexistence,
how we might stave off extinction of our species
even as we ravage the world that nurtures us

An earthworm

An earthworm pokes its pate
(or might it be its tail?)
up from the soggy lawn

all squiggly and wiggly
it squeezes through the hole
from darkness to the light

and then back down again
the slimy worm burrows
churning through the topsoil

drawing its nourishment
but also nurturing
and aerating the loam

a hermaphroditic
invertebrate creature
so different from man

the creepy night crawler
is beneficial
whereas man just destroys

The ring-necked snake

Down by our pond I lifted a flat rock:
a squirming, slithering snake startled me,
bedecked in its scaly, grey-black armor,
bright orange neck ring and underbelly—
the serpent's forked tongue darted in and out,
as if wanting to say "This is my space!"

Frightened, at first, I recoiled, then stood back
and admired my reptile friend's perfection
as it slid in silence into a hole,
escaping the human intruder me—

Just for a brief moment, I wondered at
our rather predictable responses,
both my human and the reptilian—
survival, programmed by evolution.

The traumatized turtle

I came upon a traumatized turtle
playing dead in the middle of the road—
head, legs, tail retracted under her shell,
motionless, all defenses mobilized,
frozen there with fear, in mortal danger
of being crushed to splinters, flesh and blood
by the spinning wheel of a passing truck

I did not know her direction, her goal
but gingerly picked up the armored belle
and placed her on the pond-side of the lane,
wishing that my friend would put the trial
of the traffic, of meeting a human,
all behind her and lay some eggs again.

The hummingbird

Azure and jade and gold
a hummingbird flutters
dancing to the music
sung by evolution

its slender beak seeking
the nectar of flowers
helping to spread pollen
for next summer's rebirth

its wings' rapid flapping
allowing it to float
from flower to flower
fertilizing who's next

nature, life will go on
unless our consumptive
depravity destroys
this garden of Eden

The Canada geese have landed

The Canada geese have landed
and festooned our fields with feces:
my wife attacks them with a broom,
an otherworldly scream drowns out
the cackling of the flying rats—
her shriek, like that of a banshee,
scares the unwanted fowl away.
They take off, skimming the water,
and still honking, flapping their wings,
they disappear into the sky,
as Marcia, pleased with herself,
struts slowly back up from the pond.

The birds are gone, for now, at least.

But the next year, the beasts are back,
and the game of defecating,
chasing, screeching, wing fluttering,
escaping is played out once more.

And the next year, and the next year,
the spectacle unfolds yet again:
nature's drama, while it still can.

A rafter of wild turkeys ...

A rafter of wild turkeys frolics in the field:
some toms and hens, young jakes and jennies, a few poults,
the birds strut and prance, then go pecking and poking,

they halt for a moment at the side of the road
and in a burst, vault out onto the macadam,
high-tailing it across the dangerous divide—

relief! they have made it, even the smallest chick—

bravo, say I, rooting for the rafter to live:

but ... in my gut, I, the glutton, think to myself:
would that meaty hen not have made a tasty meal?

A field mouse shares our house …

A field mouse shares our house
when we are in Vermont,
retiring discretely
to its hole in the wall,
to escape my wife's wrath.

All it wants is a crumb,
or better still, leftovers,
a warm nook in the cold,
a corner to nest in,
to give birth to its brood.

I ask my better half,
why not let the beast be?
Why set out a mousetrap,
the bloody guillotine,
to execute our friend?

The Hare

Albrecht Dürer's perfect "Young Hare"
has lived more than five hundred years,
admired in royal collections,
and now in the Albertina,
it survives with our loving care.

But hares evolved on earth more than
fifty million years ago:
will Dürer's depiction outlast
them and us as we drive most life
to unrepentant extinction?

What irony if this painting
outlives the creature it depicts
with no one left to admire it!

The seals were barking ...

The seals were barking in the night
down by the Embarcadero,
happy the tourists were not there
and they had the world to themselves

but morning comes again, too soon
and brings the swarming multitudes
with all their filth and pollution
for yet another dreary day

The Dead Coyote

(hiking in the desert)

Packing the Pushawalla trail,
across the path, in the hot sun,
we stumbled on the dead coyote:
a shot had ripped through its stomach,
then some vermin gutted the beast,
now rotting, though fur still fluffy,
redolent of fading splendor,
this once warm, sentient being
hunts the forests and fields no more

what callous thug killed it and why?

The Black Rhinoceros

(after a safari at Lewa Downs, Kenya)

The black rhinoceros is a bizarre old beast,
a crash of them on the move is a fearful sight:
loose folds of leathery skin, wrinkled and dirt-caked
sheathe that prodigious, sagging, brawny old physique
barely held off the ground by those stocky pillars;
the ungulate's keen schnozzle smells you from afar,
the floppy ears perk up to catch the faintest sound,
those half-blind peepers vainly strain to seek you out—
two slender, tapered sabers protrude from the snout,
horns worth more than gold to poachers from East Asia
who butcher these splendid endangered animals
and leave their carcasses to rot in the hot sun.
Like other magnificent species on this earth,
we have driven this creature close to extinction.

The Bear

Trekking the Royalton Turnpike,
while squashing a pesky deer fly,
I catch sight of a big black bear
crossing the road fifty yards up—
I stop in my tracks, dare not move …

A penetrating look, a wink—
ursus licks its lips, bares its teeth
at the cowering spectator
and with a wag of its buttocks,
disappears into the forest.

Polar Bears

Climate change warms the atmosphere:
the Arctic polar ice cap melts
and vainly struggles to re-form—
polar bears visit villages
along the Siberian coast;
famished, they forage for food scraps,
dig up corpses of walruses,
they cannot go out on the ice
to hunt for ringed seals and sea hares—
they are wasted, their babies die,
their habitat destroyed by man—
how long before they go extinct?

In early December 2019, about 60 polar bears were reported to have descended on the village of Ryrkaypiy in Russia's remote Chukotka region in search of food, because the sea ice was too thin for them to pursue their usual hunt.

Haiku: we plunder the seas

Uncaring stewards,
we plunder the seas for fish—
unsustainably

Haiku: glide across the sky

Glide across the sky,
glibly, behind the crest of
a pterodactyl …

III. Mankind

Elegy

Celebrate life while it lasts
before man the wise one destroys
the planter where it flowered
for this brief atom of time,

stubborn, selfish, murderous man
who cannot agree to back away
from cataclysmic consumption,
to share the commons in peace.

Homo ignoramus

Oh, stupid humankind:
Homo ignoramus,
not Homo sapiens,
should be your moniker –

you struggle to create—
you think—a better world,
your civilization:
but doing so, you sow
the seeds of its downfall

you burn fossil fuels,
chuck plastics in landfills,
use chemical poisons
to enhance farming yield,
spread your shit all over—

meanwhile, melt water from
the thawing Thwaites glacier
and the polar icecap
raises the sea level
inundating your towns
washing away your homes,
your civilization

temperatures increase:
drought burns the land, the trees,
spreads deserts, dries up lakes,

kills the vulnerable,
creates social unrest

your sibling species die,
extinction wipes them out—
for sure, you will follow …

Is it too late for you
to change your wanton ways?

When will you learn, Homo …?

When we are no longer ...

When we are no longer,
who will appreciate
what we have created:
all the works of mankind,
the beauty of our art,
the science, the knowledge
and insight in our books
the ferment of our minds
the valor of our spirit—
Mozart, Bach, Beethoven,
Vermeer and da Vinci,
Galileo, Newton,
Darwin and Aristotle
will all be forgotten
and the earth will live on
rid of the one species,
this Homo sapiens,
the destroyer of all.

Alas, my friend Darwin

To survive, to live on,
at almost any cost
is life's strongest instinct—
it must be genetic,
deep in our DNA
a potent agent of
natural selection.

But Homo sapiens
is changing the climate,
its own environment,
making much of the world
near inhospitable
for many forms of life,
sadly, including us,
as we cannot adapt,
alter our errant ways
fast enough to survive
the berserk destruction
we have unleashed on earth.

Alas, my friend Darwin,
mankind will go the way
of the woolly mammoth.

Mankind faces extinction

Like those beasts from the Jurassic,
T. rex and the pterodactyl,
mankind faces extinction—
though it is not an asteroid,
nor an erupting volcano,
but our own actions causing it:
our conspicuous consumption
and relentless pursuit of growth,
the burning of fossil fuels,
the greenhouse gas emissions
that trap the heat of the sun's rays,
melt the ice cover of the poles
and the glaciers in the mountains,
this creeping change in our climate
results in rising sea levels,
and fatal flooding on the coasts—
it brings hurricanes and flooding,
scorching drought and raging wildfires,
the rampant spread of diseases;
it destroys food crops and sources,
poisons our potable water,
leading to starvation and thirst,
creating social dislocation,
mass migration and, worse still, war—
mankind faces extinction
by our own self-centered actions

Man is a practiced, willful murderer

We kill our brother species to survive,
gluttons, we butcher them for meat to eat,
even become cannibals in dire need

We watch as famine decimates nations;
we will wage war to gain inches of land,
and nuke millions if their chiefs resist

We crucify to impose our beliefs
or send other races to gas chambers
and those who dissent to freezing gulags

We machinegun our children in their schools
and bomb civilians in shopping malls,
rampage to run them down on city streets

Man is a practiced, willful murderer,
has always been one and will never change.

We find reasons to kill ...

Why swat a fly when it flies in your face?
A mosquito that tries to bite your arm?
Why cull a crayfish that swims in your pond?
Why trap a mouse that likes to share your house?
Why shoot a fox that chews up your chickens?
Why slaughter a pig to devour its chops?
Why butcher a bull that skewers your son?
Why murder a neighbor who screws your wife?
We find reasons to kill other beings
To justify our murdering instinct
Instead of existing in peace with them.

Listen to our children

Listen to our children
who plead for their future:

they protest in the streets
and clamor for action,
for our inept leaders
to address climate change
and stop taking money
from fossil fuel firms,
those greedy producers
of vile greenhouse gases
that despoil our one world
and drive species extinct.

Listen to our children
who plead for their future!

I am sorry, my son

I

I am sorry, my son,
we have left you a mess:
we have befouled the air,
we have sullied the land,
we have warmed the oceans,
burning fossil fuels,
heating the atmosphere,
melting the polar ice.

I am sorry my son,
we have left you a mess:
we have changed the climate,
the forests are on fire,
hurricanes are raging,
flooding becomes rampant,
islands just disappear,
drought kills our crops and us.

I am sorry, my son
we have left you a mess
we have left you no time
to correct the damage,
no path to change the course,
alea iacta est,
the tipping point is past,
we will become extinct.

II

I am sorry, my son
we have left you a mess:
find another planet
to begin life again
with new and wiser ways,
save yourselves, your children,
save what remains of life,
and leave us to perish.

I am sorry, my son,
we have left you a mess:
we are the guilty ones.

The Nutcracker

It's Christmas Eve, a roaring fire,
but instead of Clara's dream world
of Drosselmeier's Nutcracker
who defeats a rodent army
led by the Mouse King in battle
then turns into a handsome prince
to take her to the Land of Sweets
ruled by the Sugar Plum Fairy,
my dream is of a healthy world
a world where we can breathe clean air
and drink unpolluted water,
where we all get enough to eat,
where civilians are not bombed
and there is no war, no killing—
but I know there is no such world
and there never will be again.

When I no longer care about the world

When I no longer care about the world,
no longer rage against the rape of earth,
the wanton killing of other species,

When I no longer hear those cello's tears,
nor see the setting sun paint the heavens,
or at night, play with words to write this poem,

When I am too tired to taste your cooking,
or my palate is too numb for some wine,
or to savor the flesh of a fresh fig,

When I can no longer talk to my kids,
or when I become too grumpy to play
canasta or war with my grandchildren,

When I do not feel the thrill of your touch,
or no longer yearn for your sensual kiss,
for that one last loving, beguiling smile,

Maggots gnaw then at the still living brain,
my mind creeps slowly into the black hole:
and I care not about this messed up world.

Cello's Tears is the title of my first poetry collection, published by P.R.A. Publishing in 2015.

Maybe eons from now

Maybe eons from now
when Homo sapiens
is an extinct species,
some feeling mind substance
from another planet
will find my skull and bones,
dust it off and marvel
at this strange organism
that razed its earthly home,
annihilating life.

Can we not change our ways?

Or is it just too late?

Crepuscular shadows

Crepuscular shadows cavort on the wall,
pirouetting in a ballet of rot
choreographed by Emperor Nero,
Caligula and leaders of their ilk,
who fiddle as wildfires scorch mother earth
and floods and storms ravage our sustenance.

These kings are self-centered, and like Midas,
give all to get gold to add to their hoards
and pursue perverse, illicit pleasures,
while drought destroys our crops, our children starve,
our trails and roads become raging rivers
and our homes and cities are washed away.

What future is there for my grandchildren?
What hope is there for human life on earth?

A coterie of criminals

A coterie of criminals
has usurped our governments,
destroyed our democracies
and ruined our institutions:
Messrs. Trump, Putin and Modi,
Xi Jingpin and Bolsonaro,
Erdogan, Orban, Kim Jong-un,
Netanyahu and still others—
they are all lying oligarchs
and only in it for themselves
and their fellow exploiting pigs.

They do not care about the earth,
the fragile state of our planet,
nor about the poor, the needy,
the working or the middle class—
they do not spare a fleeting thought
for the future of our children:
it is time for us to rise up
and grab power for the people!

Sometimes I wish I could just close my eyes

Sometimes I wish I could just close my eyes
and drift peacefully into nothingness,
away from this troubled, polluted world,
where too many of us humans compete,
like piglets suckling on mother earth's teats,
to grow fat on those riches we extract
or just to survive while our brothers starve.
We rampage across the land in our cars,
pickup trucks, RVs, sometimes even tanks,
trample plants, cut down trees, dig for metals;
we chuck our plastic waste into the sea
to join the feces floating down sewers
and spew chemicals and particulates
into the life sustaining atmosphere.
I would be happy to negate all this,
but there is no turning back, no escape
to a world untouched by depraved mankind:
we must wallow in the mire we have forged
and suffer as our frail bodies expire
and earth mutates into a lifeless sphere.

Haiku: you had a good run

You had a good run,
man, the murdering species—
you fucked up the world

Haiku: pills can prolong life

Pills can prolong life,
even improve it for some—
or just end it all

Haiku: a good friend is gone

A good friend is gone,
leaving those who loved her behind
with grief in their hearts

Haiku: the samurai

The samurai
disembowels his body
with his katana

Haiku: as friends age and die

As friends age and die
and the world withers with use
I too decompose

Haiku: bloodstains on the sheet

bloodstains on the sheet
still remind me of your death
only yesterday

IV. Pandemic

There are too many of us on this earth ...

There are too many of us on this earth,
far too many consuming human beasts
who exploit and squander its resources—
self-centered, ignorant creatures who cause,
then deny catastrophic climate change.
Some even feign concern but do nothing.
Our leaders promote Gaia's abuse,
we all pursue our lives at her expense.
But now our tormented planet fights back—
drought desiccates the soil, killing our crops,
wildfires burn forests and threaten our towns,
ice melts and the seas surge, swamping our shores,
a virulent virus wipes out the old,
our social fabric frays, then tears apart,
we fight among ourselves for living space,
for food and clean water, breathable air.
As in every war, casualties mount,
flora and fauna species are wiped out,
and humankind, too, faces extinction.
A much-changed mother earth will still live on
but without its perverse, destructive child.

Angry Gaia fights back ...

Angry Gaia fights back
with vengeance, unleashing
a virulent virus,
a global pandemic
on the errant children
who violated her.
Now these all-knowing beasts
are lost: they cannot cope,
they beg for her mercy.

Tanka: Is our world ending?

Is our world ending?
Earth has unleashed a virus
to punish mankind:
the wanton depravity
of our Ponzi consumption
degrades the natural world.

We, who think we are earthly gods ...

We, who think we are earthly gods,
we are being decimated
by a miniscule enemy
a wild beast that spreads like wildfire
the novel Corona virus:
stay six feet away, do not cough,
do not touch anything at all
scrub your hands, use sanitizer—
we are afraid to go outside,
the economy has been ruined
and we are now all unemployed.
What kind of life is this for gods?

We breathe clean air again

Our economy has gone moribund:
factories no longer spew those gases
that wreak havoc on our lungs, cause cancer;
we do not drive our obscene gas guzzlers—
we breathe clean air again, like we once did—
for now: but tell me, how long will this last?
Is it just while this pandemic rages,
killing the old and those vulnerable,
or will we have learned how to spare our earth?

A Doctor's Dilemma

In an otherworldly stupor
I survey the ICU ward—
as the epidemic explodes,
COVID-19 exacts its toll:
the unwell entombed in their beds,
sucking life-sustaining oxygen
out of those scarce ventilators,
monitors flashing and ringing,
each grim breath a fight to survive
until the next, or the very last.

I dread the coming invasion,
when I will be forced to play god,
and decide who gets the machine
just freed up as another corpse
is wheeled away to the morgue:
the diabetic and deaf child,
the uncompromised grandfather
or the mother with breast cancer,
while I send the rest to the grave.
This is not what a doctor does:
I am an executioner.

Thank you to my friend Christina Starobin for the title suggestion.

Questions of the Virus

With travel so risky
will our children ever
come and see us again?

Will we be together
to celebrate Christmas,
or each other's birthdays,

Will all our grandchildren
come and swim in our pond,
play soccer on our lawn,

Will they have memories
of fun shared times with us,
the laughter, all the joy?

Or will the vile virus
work to diminish us,
forbid the human touch
that says, I love you son,
my daughter, my grandchild—
will it banish the smile
of happiness at being
with those you love the most?

Haiku: a pandemic looms

From Wuhan, China,
the coronavirus kills:
a pandemic looms

Haiku: the bat and the pangolin

We abuse nature—
the bat and the pangolin,
their virus kills us

Haiku: what will save us?

What will save us?
Social distancing, they say
Fight the pandemic!

Haiku: virus goes viral

Virus goes viral
not enough ventilators
death toll grows daily

About the Author

Born in Budapest, Geza Tatrallyay escaped with his family from Communist Hungary in 1956 during the Revolution, immigrating to Canada. After attending the University of Toronto Schools and serving as School Captain in his last year, he graduated with a B.A. in Human Ecology from Harvard College in 1972, and, as a Rhodes Scholar from Ontario, obtained a B.A. / M.A. in Human Sciences from Oxford University in 1974. He completed his studies with a M.Sc. from London School of Economics and Politics in 1975. Geza worked as a host in the Ontario Pavilion at Expo 70 in Osaka, Japan, and represented Canada in epée fencing at the Montreal Olympics in 1976. His professional experience has included stints in government, international finance and environmental entrepreneurship. Geza is a citizen of Canada and Hungary, and as a green card holder, currently divides his time between Barnard, Vermont and San Francisco. He is married to Marcia, and their daughter, Alexandra, lives in San Francisco with husband David, and two sons, Sebastian, and Orlando, while their son, Nicholas, lives in Nairobi with his Hungarian wife, Fanni and daughter Sophia.

Geza's poems have been published in many different literary journals in Canada and the USA over the years. A collection of his poems, *Cello's Tears,* was published in May 2015 by P.R.A. Publishing, and another poetry collection, *Sighs and Murmurs,* was released in April of 2018 by the same publisher. *Extinction,* his third volume of poems was published by P.R.A. Publishing in April 2019. *Extinction Rebellion* is his fourth collection.

Geza's thriller, *Twisted Reasons,* the first book in the 'Twisted Trilogy' of international crime thrillers, was published in December 2014 by Deux Voiliers Publishing. The second book in the series, *Twisted Traffick,* was released in October 2017 by Black Opal Books, and the third book, *Twisted Fates,* was published by Black Opal Books in June 2018. An international political thriller set in France, *The Rainbow Vintner,* was published by Black Opal Books in February 2019. Earlier, Geza self-published an e-thriller, *Arctic Meltdown,* now available through Amazon, with a second edition in paperback format to be released during 2020.

Geza has also written three memoirs. *For the Children,* the story of his family's escape from Communist Hungary and immigration to Canada in 1956 was published in 2015 by Editions Dedicaces. His second memoir, *The Expo Affair,* the story of three Czechoslovak girls who approached him for help to defect at the world's fair in Osaka, Japan in 1970 was published in 2016 by Guernica Editions under their MiroLand imprint. *The Fencers*, the third book in Geza's 'Cold War Escape Trilogy' – about a Romanian-Hungarian fencer who approached him to help him defect at the Montreal Olympics – was published in March 2019.

Geza's first children's picture storybook, *The Waffle and the Pancake,* was published in September 2018 by Bayeux Arts. He has a second children's book, *How Rudolf's Nose Turned Red,* seeking publication.

Geza's first collection of short stories, *The Spinning Mind*, will be brought out by P.R.A. Publishing in the summer of 2020.

9 789390 202324